Purposeful
Vision
Journal

Rita Brown

Mission: To Proclaim Transformation and Truth
Publisher: Transformed Publishing, Cocoa, FL
Website: www.transformedpublishing.com
Email: transformedpublishing@gmail.com

ISBN: 978-1-953241-57-3 (paperback)

ISBN: 978-1-953241-58-0 (hardcover)

To: _____
From: _____
Date: _____

You have not, because you ask not.

You lust and do not have. You murder and covet and cannot obtain. You fight and war. Yet you do not have because you do not ask.

-James 4:2

As we begin our journey together to fulfill purpose with clear vision, I must start by sharing

My Why!

The Lord has equipped each of us with our own talents. Although, He has equipped us, if we do not take the first step, being equipped has no value. By taking the first step we are trusting God by faith and that is *My Why*.

What is Faith, you ask?

Faith is the substance of things hoped for and the evidence of things not seen (*see* Hebrews 11:1).

God will never bring us to anything that He will not bring us through. So to tie it all together, *My Why,* is simply because God is the author and the finisher of my Faith, who for the joy that was set before Him endured the cross, despising the shame, and is sat down at the right hand of the throne of God. For consider Him who endured such contradiction of sinners against Himself, lest ye be worried and faint in your minds (*see* Hebrews 12:2-3).

When I hear from God I am compelled to move because I know that if He gives me a command (vision) that the provision will follow.

"God is not a man, that He should lie,
Nor a son of man, that He should repent.
Has He said, and will He not do?
Or has He spoken, and will He not make it good?["]
-Numbers 23:19

So, I know without a shadow of doubt that everything I put my hands to shall prosper! Again, why not me? Be Blessed!

They shall not be ashamed in the evil time,
And in the days of famine they shall be satisfied.
-Psalm 37:19

"The Spirit of the Lord is upon Me, because He has anointed Me
To preach the gospel to *the* poor; He has sent Me to heal *the*
brokenhearted, To proclaim liberty to *the* captives
And recovery of sight to the blind,
To set at liberty those who are oppressed;["]
-Luke 4:18

[A]nd *when* your herds and your flocks multiply, and your silver and your gold are multiplied, and all that you have is multiplied;
-Deuteronomy 8:13

"And you shall remember the Lord your God, for *it is* He who gives you power to get wealth, that He may establish His covenant which He swore to your fathers, as *it is* this day.
-Deuteronomy 8:18

The thief does not come except to steal, and to kill, and to destroy. I have come that they may have life, and that they may have *it* more abundantly.
-John 10:10

And God *is* able to make all grace abound toward you,
that you, always having all sufficiency in all *things*,
may have an abundance for every good work.
-2 Corinthians 9:8

Beloved, I pray that you may prosper in all things
and be in health, just as your soul prospers.
-3 John 1:2

Unless the Lord builds the house, they labor in vain who build it;
Unless the Lord guards the city, the watchman stays awake in vain.
-Psalm 127:1

I returned and saw under the sun that—the race is not to the swift,
Nor the battle to the strong, nor bread to the wise,
Nor riches to men of understanding, nor favor to men of skill;
But time and chance happen to them all.
-Ecclesiastes 9:11

"While the earth remains, seedtime and harvest,
Cold and heat, winter and summer,
And day and night shall not cease."
-Genesis 8:22

So Jesus answered and said to them, "Have faith in God.["]
-Mark 11:22

So then faith *comes* by hearing, and hearing by the word of God.
-Romans 10:17

Now may He who supplies seed to the sower,
and bread for food, supply and multiply the seed you
have *sown* and increase the fruits of your righteousness,
-2 Corinthians 9:10

Let your light so shine before men, that they may see your
good works and glorify your Father in heaven.
-Matthew 5:16

But those who wait on the Lord
Shall renew their strength;
They shall mount up with wings like eagles,
They shall run and not be weary,
They shall walk and not faint.
-Isaiah 40:31

"[B]ut if I do, though you do not believe Me, believe the works, that you may know and believe that the Father is in Me, and I in Him."
-John 10:38

Now when He was asked by the Pharisees when the kingdom
of God would come, He answered them and said,
"The kingdom of God does not come with observation;["]
-Luke 17:20

Blessed *be* the God and Father of our Lord Jesus Christ, who has blessed us with every spiritual blessing in the heavenly *places* in Christ,
-Ephesians 1:3

[B]ut glory, honor, and peace to everyone who works
what is good, to the Jew first and also to the Greek.
-Romans 2:10

"I know your works. See, I have set before you an open door,
and no one can shut it; for you have a little strength,
have kept My word, and have not denied My name.["]
-Revelation 3:8

But he who looks into the perfect law of liberty and continues *in it*,
and is not a forgetful hearer but a doer of the work,
this one will be blessed in what he does.
-James 1:25

And of His fullness we have all received, and grace for grace.
-John 1:16

And the younger of them said to *his* father, 'Father, give me the portion of goods that falls *to me*.' So he divided to them *his* livelihood.
-Luke 15:12

Thanks *be* to God for His indescribable gift!
-2 Corinthians 9:15

But as you abound in everything—in faith, in speech, in knowledge, in all diligence, and in your love for us—*see* that you abound in this grace also.
-2 Corinthians 8:7

"Will a man rob God? Yet you have robbed Me!
But you say, 'In what way have we robbed You?'
In tithes and offerings.["]
-Malachi 3:8

[A]lthough I was formerly a blasphemer, a persecutor, and an insolent man; but I obtained mercy because I did it ignorantly in unbelief.
-1 Timothy 1:13

Immediately the father of the child cried out and said with tears,
"Lord, I believe; help my unbelief!"
-Mark 9:24

And when He had called His twelve disciples to *Him*,
He gave them power *over* unclean spirits, to cast them out,
and to heal all kinds of sickness and all kinds of disease.
-Matthew 10:1

Now this is the confidence that we have in Him,
that if we ask anything according to His will, He hears us.
-1 John 5:14

And His name, through faith in His name, has made this man strong, whom you see and know. Yes, the faith which *comes* through Him has given him this perfect soundness in the presence of you all.
-Acts 3:16

Be sober, be vigilant; because your adversary the devil walks
about like a roaring lion, seeking whom he may devour.
-1 Peter 5:8

And the God of peace will crush Satan under your feet shortly.
The grace of our Lord Jesus Christ *be* with you. Amen.
-Romans 16:20

The fear of the Lord *is* the beginning of wisdom;
A good understanding have all those who do *His commandments*.
His praise endures forever.
-Psalm 111:10

[B]ecause he did not know what to say, for they were greatly afraid.
-Mark 9:6

_____
_____
_____
_____
_____
_____
_____
_____
_____
_____
_____
_____
_____
_____
_____
_____
_____
_____
_____
_____
_____
_____
_____
_____
_____
_____
_____
_____

If any of you lacks wisdom, let him ask of God,
who gives to all liberally and without reproach,
and it will be given to him.
-James 1:5

Listen to counsel and receive instruction,
That you may be wise in your latter days.
-Proverbs 19:20

Therefore, since we are receiving a kingdom which cannot be shaken,
let us have grace, by which we may serve God
acceptably with reverence and godly fear.
-Hebrews 12:28

For we are the circumcision, who worship God in the Spirit,
rejoice in Christ Jesus, and have no confidence in the flesh,
-Philippians 3:3

And to one he gave five talents, to another two, and to another one,
to each according to his own ability;
and immediately he went on a journey.
-Matthew 25:15

I beseech you therefore, brethren, by the mercies of God,
that you present your bodies a living sacrifice, holy,
acceptable to God, *which is* your reasonable service.
-Romans 12:1

For whoever finds me finds life,
And obtains favor from the Lord;
-Proverbs 8:35

God *is* Spirit,
and those who worship Him must worship in spirit and truth."
-John 4:24

I know that whatever God does, it shall be forever.
Nothing can be added to it, and nothing taken from it.
God does *it*, that men should fear before Him.
-Ecclesiastes 3:14

For wisdom *is* better than rubies,
And all the things one may desire cannot be compared with her.
-Proverbs 8:11

_____
_____
_____
_____
_____
_____
_____
_____
_____
_____
_____
_____
_____
_____
_____
_____
_____
_____
_____
_____
_____
_____
_____
_____
_____
_____
_____

Establish Your word to Your servant,
Who is *devoted* to fearing You.
-Psalm 119:38

For I know the thoughts that I think toward you, says the Lord,
thoughts of peace and not of evil, to give you a future and a hope.
-Jeremiah 29:11

The Lord *is* good,
A stronghold in the day of trouble;
And He knows those who trust in Him.
-Nahum 1:7

The wise shall inherit glory,
But shame shall be the legacy of fools.
-Proverbs 3:35

"Do not fear, little flock,
for it is your Father's good pleasure to give you the kingdom.["]
-Luke 12:32

But as it is written: "Eye has not seen, nor ear heard,
Nor have entered into the heart of man
The things which God has prepared for those who love Him."
-1 Corinthians 2:9

Death and life *are* in the power of the tongue,
And those who love it will eat its fruit.
-Proverbs 18:21

Oh, taste and see that the Lord *is* good;
Blessed *is* the man *who* trusts in Him!
-Psalm 34:8

_____

_____

_____

_____

_____

_____

_____

_____

_____

_____

_____

_____

_____

_____

_____

_____

_____

_____

_____

_____

_____

_____

_____

[T]he voice of joy and the voice of gladness, the voice of the
bridegroom and the voice of the bride, the voice of those who will say:
"Praise the Lord of hosts, for the Lord is good,
For His mercy *endures* forever"—
and of those *who will* bring the sacrifice of praise into the
house of the Lord. For I will cause the captives of
the land to return as at the first,' says the Lord.
-Jeremiah 33:11

The heart of the wise teaches his mouth,
And adds learning to his lips.
-Proverbs 16:23

Give unto the Lord the glory due to His name;
Worship the Lord in the beauty of holiness.
-Psalm 29:2

Keep your tongue from evil,
And your lips from speaking deceit.
-Psalm 34:13

A wise *man* will hear and increase learning,
And a man of understanding will attain wise counsel,
-Proverbs 1:5

For the vision *is* yet for an appointed time;
But at the end it will speak, and it will not lie.
Though it tarries, wait for it;
Because it will surely come, it will not tarry.
-Habakkuk 2:3

After these things the word of the Lord came to Abram in a vision,
saying, "Do not be afraid, Abram. I *am* your shield,
your exceedingly great reward."
-Genesis 15:1

For God has not given us a spirit of fear,
but of power and of love and of a sound mind.
-2 Timothy 1:7

[C]asting down arguments and every high thing that exalts itself
against the knowledge of God, bringing every thought
into captivity to the obedience of Christ,
-2 Corinthians 10:5

And do not be conformed to this world, but be transformed
by the renewing of your mind, that you may prove what is that
good and acceptable and perfect will of God.
-Romans 12:2

For as he thinks in his heart, so *is* he.
"Eat and drink!" he says to you,
But his heart is not with you.
-Proverbs 23:7

The plans of the diligent *lead* surely to plenty,
But *those* of everyone *who* is hasty, surely to poverty.
-Proverbs 21:5

Finally, brethren, whatever things are true, whatever things *are* noble, whatever things *are* just, whatever things *are* pure, whatever things *are* lovely, whatever things *are* of good report, if *there* is any virtue and if *there* is anything praiseworthy—meditate on these things.
-Philippians 4:8

Let the words of my mouth and the meditation of my heart
Be acceptable in Your sight, O Lord, my strength and my Redeemer.
-Psalm 19:14

A man has joy by the answer of his mouth,
And a word *spoken* in due season, how good *it is*!
-Proverbs 15:23

The mouth of the righteous *is* a well of life,
But violence covers the mouth of the wicked.
-Proverbs 10:11

Set a guard, O Lord, over my mouth;
Keep watch over the door of my lips.
-Psalm 141:3

Then David put garrisons in Syria of Damascus;
and the Syrians became David's servants, *and* brought tribute.
So the Lord preserved David wherever he went.
-2 Samuel 8:6

Yet in all these things we are more than conquerors
through Him who loved us.
-Romans 8:37

Yours, O Lord, *is* the greatness, the power and the glory,
The victory and the majesty; for all *that is* in heaven and in earth is Yours;
Yours *is* the kingdom, O Lord, and You are exalted as head over all.
-1 Chronicles 29:11

For the Lord takes pleasure in His people;
He will beautify the humble with salvation.
-Psalm 149:4

A feast is made for laughter, and wine makes merry;
But money answers everything.
-Ecclesiastes 10:19

The blessing of the Lord makes *one* rich,
And He adds no sorrow with it.
-Proverbs 10:22

But without faith *it is* impossible to please *Him*,
for he who comes to God must believe *that* He is,
and that He is a rewarder of those who diligently seek Him.
-Hebrews 11:6

But from there you will seek the Lord your God, and you will find *Him* if you seek Him with all your heart and with all your soul.
-Deuteronomy 4:29

If then you were raised with Christ,
seek those things which are above, where Christ is,
sitting at the right hand of God.
-Colossians 3:1

[I]f My people who are called by My name will humble themselves, and pray and seek My face, and turn from their wicked ways, then I will hear from heaven, and will forgive their sin and heal their land.
-2 Chronicles 7:14

I can of Myself do nothing. As I hear, I judge;
and My judgment is righteous, because I do not seek
My own will but the will of the Father who sent Me.
-John 5:30

_____

_____

_____

_____

_____

_____

_____

_____

_____

_____

_____

_____

_____

_____

_____

_____

_____

_____

_____

_____

_____

_____

_____

One thing I have desired of the Lord, that will I seek:
That I may dwell in the house of the Lord
All the days of my life,
To behold the beauty of the Lord,
And to inquire in His temple.
-Psalm 27:4

But seek first the kingdom of God and His righteousness,
and all these things shall be added to you.
-Matthew 6:33

The Lord *is* good to those who wait for Him,
To the soul *who* seeks Him.
-Lamentations 3:25

"Now acquaint yourself with Him, and be at peace;
Thereby good will come to you.["]
-Job 22:21

Pursue peace with all *people*, and holiness,
without which no one will see the Lord:
-Hebrews 12:14

Peace I leave with you, My peace I give to you; not as the world gives
do I give to you. Let not your heart be troubled, neither let it be afraid.
-John 14:27

When a man's ways please the Lord,
He makes even his enemies to be at peace with him.
-Proverbs 16:7

[A]nd the peace of God, which surpasses all understanding,
will guard your hearts and minds through Christ Jesus.
-Philippians 4:7

You will keep *him* in perfect peace,
Whose mind is stayed *on You,*
Because he trusts in You.
-Isaiah 26:3

["]But you shall receive power when the Holy Spirit has come upon you; and you shall be witnesses to Me in Jerusalem, and in all Judea and Samaria, and to the end of the earth."
-Acts 1:8

Behold, I give you the authority to trample on serpents and scorpions,
and over all the power of the enemy,
and nothing shall by any means hurt you.
-Luke 10:19

'The silver is Mine, and the gold is Mine,' says the Lord of hosts.
-Haggai 2:8

[T]hat He would grant you, according to the riches of His glory, to be strengthened with might through His Spirit in the inner man,
-Ephesians 3:16

I waited patiently for the Lord; and He inclined to me,
And heard my cry.
-Psalm 40:1

The end of a thing *is* better than its beginning;
The patient in spirit *is* better than the proud in spirit.
-Ecclesiastes 7:8

And let us not grow weary while doing good,
for in due season we shall reap if we do not lose heart.
-Galatians 6:9

Because you have kept My command to persevere, I also will keep you from the hour of trial which shall come upon the whole world, to test those who dwell on the earth.
-Revelation 3:10

[T]hat by two immutable things, in which it *is* impossible for God to lie, we might have strong consolation, who have fled for refuge to lay hold of the hope set before *us.*
-Hebrews 6:18

The Lord also will be a refuge for the oppressed,
A refuge in times of trouble.
-Psalm 9:9

In the fear of the Lord *there is* strong confidence,
And His children will have a place of refuge.
-Proverbs 14:26

The eternal God *is your* refuge,
And underneath *are* the everlasting arms;
He will thrust out the enemy from before you,
And will say, 'Destroy!'
-Deuteronomy 33:27

Beloved, I pray that you may prosper in all things
and be in health, just as your soul prospers.
-3 John 2

And my God shall supply all your need according
to His riches in glory by Christ Jesus.
-Philippians 4:19

["]Bring all the tithes into the storehouse,
That there may be food in My house,
And try Me now in this," says the Lord of hosts,
"If I will not open for you the windows of heaven
And pour out for you *such* blessing
That *there will* not be *room* enough to *receive it.*["]
-Malachi 3:10

And when he observed him, he was afraid, and said, "What is it, lord?"
So he said to him, "Your prayers and your alms have
come up for a memorial before God.["]
-Acts 10:4

"As the Father loved Me, I also have loved you; abide in My love.["]
-John 15:9

And walk in love, as Christ also has loved us and given Himself for us,
an offering and a sacrifice to God for a sweet-smelling aroma.
-Ephesians 5:2

And we have known and believed the love that God has for us.
God is love, and he who abides in love abides in God, and God in him.
-1 John 4:16

We love Him because He first loved us.
-1 John 4:19

[B]ut, speaking the truth in love,
may grow up in all things into Him who is the head—Christ—
-Ephesians 4:15

Now hope does not disappoint, because the love of God has been
poured out in our hearts by the Holy Spirit who was given to us.
-Romans 5:5

Then He spoke a parable to them,
that men always ought to pray and not lose heart,
-Luke 18:1

Until now you have asked nothing in My name.
Ask, and you will receive, that your joy may be full.
-John 16:24

Seek the Lord while He may be found,
Call upon Him while He is near.
-Isaiah 55:6

You will make your prayer to Him,
He will hear you, and you will pay your vows.
-Job 22:27

Lead me in Your truth and teach me,
For You *are* the God of my salvation;
On You I wait all the day.
-Psalm 25:5

Therefore the Lord will wait, that He may be gracious to you;
And therefore He will be exalted, that He may have mercy on you.
For the Lord *is* a God of justice;
Blessed *are* all those who wait for Him.
-Isaiah 30:18

Fight the good fight of faith, lay hold on eternal life,
to which you were also called and have confessed the
good confession in the presence of many witnesses.
-1 Timothy 6:12

"The Lord will cause your enemies who rise against you
to be defeated before your face; they shall come out
against you one way and flee before you seven ways.["]
-Deuteronomy 28:7

By your patience possess your souls.
-Luke 21:19

A wrathful man stirs up strife,
But *he who is* slow to anger allays contention.
-Proverbs 15:18

When you make a vow to God, do not delay to pay it;
For *He has* no pleasure in fools.
Pay what you have vowed—
-Ecclesiastes 5:4

Do not hasten in your spirit to be angry,
For anger rests in the bosom of fools.
-Ecclesiastes 7:9

Let us therefore come boldly to the throne of grace,
that we may obtain mercy and find grace to help in time of need.
-Hebrews 4:16

_____
_____
_____
_____
_____
_____
_____
_____
_____
_____
_____
_____
_____
_____
_____
_____
_____
_____
_____
_____
_____
_____
_____
_____
_____
_____
_____

You have granted me life and favor,
And Your care has preserved my spirit.
-Job 10:12

But He gives more grace. Therefore He says:
"God resists the proud, but gives grace to the humble."
-James 4:6

[A]fter John had first preached, before His coming,
the baptism of repentance to all the people of Israel.
-Acts 13:24

For by grace you have been saved through faith,
and that not of yourselves; *it is* the gift of God,
-Ephesians 2:8

But the free gift *is* not like the offense. For if by the one man's offense
many died, much more the grace of God and the gift by the grace
of the one Man, Jesus Christ, abounded to many.
-Romans 5:15

For You *are* the glory of their strength,
And in Your favor our horn is exalted.
-Psalm 89:17

Blessed *are* those who mourn,
For they shall be comforted.
-Matthew 5:4

Therefore gird up the loins of your mind, be sober,
and rest *your* hope fully upon the grace that is to be brought
to you at the revelation of Jesus Christ;
-1 Peter 1:13

[T]he eyes of your understanding being enlightened;
that you may know what is the hope of His calling,
what are the riches of the glory of His inheritance in the saints,
-Ephesians 1:18

Now may the God of hope fill you with all joy and peace in believing,
that you may abound in hope by the power of the Holy Spirit.
-Romans 15:13

_____
_____
_____
_____
_____
_____
_____
_____
_____
_____
_____
_____
_____
_____
_____
_____
_____
_____
_____
_____
_____
_____
_____
_____
_____
_____
_____

Hope deferred makes the heart sick,
But *when* the desire comes, *it is* a tree of life.
-Proverbs 13:12

Now when the congregation had broken up, many of the Jews
and devout proselytes followed Paul and Barnabas, who, speaking
to them, persuaded them to continue in the grace of God.
-Acts 13:43

For the Lord God is a sun and shield;
The Lord will give grace and glory;
No good *thing* will He withhold
From those who walk uprightly.
-Psalm 84:11

And He said to me, "My grace is sufficient for you, for My strength is made perfect in weakness." Therefore most gladly I will rather boast in my infirmities, that the power of Christ may rest upon me.
-2 Corinthians 12:9

For You, O Lord, will bless the righteous;
With favor You will surround him as *with* a shield.
-Psalm 5:12

So we may boldly say:
"The Lord *is* my helper; I will not fear.
What can man do to me?"
-Hebrews 13:6

Then she came and worshiped Him, saying, "Lord, help me!"
-Matthew 15:25

This Book of the Law shall not depart from your mouth, but you shall meditate in it day and night, that you may observe to do according to all that is written in it. For then you will make your way prosperous, and then you will have good success.
-Joshua 1:8

_____
_____
_____
_____
_____
_____
_____
_____
_____
_____
_____
_____
_____
_____
_____
_____
_____
_____
_____
_____
_____
_____
_____
_____
_____
_____
_____

Have I not commanded you? Be strong and of good courage;
do not be afraid, nor be dismayed,
for the Lord your God *is* with you wherever you go."
-Joshua 1:9

But immediately Jesus spoke to them, saying,
"Be of good cheer! It is I; do not be afraid."
-Matthew 14:27

Be of good courage,
And He shall strengthen your heart,
All you who hope in the Lord.
-Psalm 31:24

For in the time of trouble He shall hide me in His pavilion;
In the secret place of His tabernacle He shall hide me;
He shall set me high upon a rock.
-Psalm 27:5

I will be glad and rejoice in Your mercy,
For You have considered my trouble;
You have known my soul in adversities,
-Psalm 31:7

Therefore I will look to the Lord;
I will wait for the God of my salvation;
My God will hear me.
-Micah 7:7

He only *is* my rock and my salvation;
He is my defense; I shall not be greatly moved.
-Psalm 62:2

But the fruit of the Spirit is love, joy, peace,
longsuffering, kindness, goodness, faithfulness,
-Galatians 5:22

Trust in the Lord, and do good;
Dwell in the land, and feed on His faithfulness.
-Psalm 37:3

For assuredly, I say to you, whoever says to this mountain,
'Be removed and be cast into the sea,' and does not doubt in his heart,
but believes that those things he says will be done,
he will have whatever he says.
-Mark 11:23

So Jesus said to them, "Because of your unbelief; for assuredly,
I say to you, if you have faith as a mustard seed, you will say to this
mountain, 'Move from here to there,' and it will move;
and nothing will be impossible for you.["]
-Matthew 17:20

["]Be strong and of good courage, do not fear nor be afraid of them;
for the Lord your God, He is the One who goes with you.
He will not leave you nor forsake you."
-Deuteronomy 31:6

Therefore, my beloved brethren, be steadfast, immovable,
always abounding in the work of the Lord,
knowing that your labor is not in vain in the Lord.
-1 Corinthians 15:58

Therefore do not cast away your confidence, which has great reward.
-Hebrews 10:35

My heart is steadfast, O God, my heart is steadfast;
I will sing and give praise.
-Psalm 57:7

[C]asting all your care upon Him, for He cares for you.
-1 Peter 5:7

[A]nd the cares of this world, the deceitfulness of riches,
and the desires for other things entering in choke the word,
and it becomes unfruitful.
-Mark 4:19

And they cast out many demons,
and anointed with oil many who were sick, and healed *them*.
-Mark 6:13

But the anointing which you have received from Him abides in you,
and you do not need that anyone teach you; but as the same
anointing teaches you concerning all things, and is true,
and is not a lie, and just as it has taught you, you will abide in Him.
-1 John 2:27

Do not be afraid of sudden terror,
Nor of trouble from the wicked when it comes;
-Proverbs 3:25

Which of you by worrying can add one cubit to his stature?
-Matthew 6:27

"The Spirit of the Lord God is upon Me,
Because the Lord has anointed Me
To preach good tidings to the poor;
He has sent Me to heal the brokenhearted,
To proclaim liberty to the captives,
And the opening of the prison to *those who are* bound;["]
-Isaiah 61:1

But you have an anointing from the Holy One, and you know all things.
-1 John 2:20

But Peter and the *other* apostles answered and said:
"We ought to obey God rather than men.["]
-Acts 5:29

_____

_____

_____

_____

_____

_____

_____

_____

_____

_____

_____

_____

_____

_____

_____

_____

_____

_____

_____

_____

_____

_____

_____

_____

_____

For do I now persuade men, or God? Or do I seek to please men?
For if I still pleased men, I would not be a bondservant of Christ.
-Galatians 1:10

Thus also faith by itself, if it does not have works, is dead.
-James 2:17

[T]hrough whom also we have access by faith into this grace
in which we stand, and rejoice in hope of the glory of God.
-Romans 5:2

Sacrifice and offering You did not desire;
My ears You have opened.
Burnt offering and sin offering You did not require.
-Psalm 40:6

"Now it shall come to pass, if you diligently obey the voice of the Lord your God, to observe carefully all His commandments which I command you today, that the Lord your God will set you high above all nations of the earth.["]
-Deuteronomy 28:1

For to this *end* we both labor and suffer reproach,
because we trust in the living God, who is *the* Savior of all men,
especially of those who believe.
-1 Timothy 4:10

["]The people who sat in darkness have seen a great light, and upon those who sat in the region and shadow of death Light has dawned."
-Matthew 4:16

A new commandment I give to you, that you love one another;
as I have loved you, that you also love one another.
-John 13:34

No one has seen God at any time. If we love one another,
God abides in us, and His love has been perfected in us.
-1 John 4:12

For thus says the Lord God, the Holy One of Israel:
"In returning and rest you shall be saved;
In quietness and confidence shall be your strength.". . .
Isaiah 30:15

And again:
"I will put My trust in Him."
And again:
"Here am I and the children whom God has given Me."
-Hebrews 2:13

"So you shall serve the Lord your God,
and He will bless your bread and your water.
And I will take sickness away from the midst of you.["]
Exodus 23:25

_____

_____

_____

_____

_____

_____

_____

_____

_____

_____

_____

_____

_____

_____

_____

_____

_____

_____

_____

_____

_____

_____

_____

_____

_____

[']For I will restore health to you
And heal you of your wounds,' says the Lord,
'Because they called you an outcast *saying*:
"This *is* Zion; no one seeks her."
-Jeremiah 30:17

"Behold the proud,
His soul is not upright in him;
But the just shall live by his faith.["]
-Habakkuk 2:4

I press toward the goal for the prize
of the upward call of God in Christ Jesus.
-Philippians 3:14

"For the Lord God will help Me;
Therefore I will not be disgraced;
Therefore I have set My face like a flint,
And I know that I will not be ashamed.["]
-Isaiah 50:7

_____
_____
_____
_____
_____
_____
_____
_____
_____
_____
_____
_____
_____
_____
_____
_____
_____
_____
_____
_____
_____
_____
_____
_____
_____
_____
_____
_____
_____

The Lord *is* my strength and my shield;
My heart trusted in Him, and I am helped;
Therefore my heart greatly rejoices,
And with my song I will praise Him.
-Psalm 28:7